D0760561

NAILING DOWN A BOARD

NAILING DOWN A BOARD

Serving Effectively on the Not-for-Profit Board

Charles C. Ryrie

kregel
PUBLICATIONS

Grand Rapids, MI 49501

Nailing Down a Board: Serving Effectively on the Not-for-Profit Board

Published by Kregel Publications, a division of Kregel, Inc., P.O. Box 2607, Grand Rapids, MI 49501. Kregel Publications provides trusted, biblical publications for Christian growth and service. Your comments and suggestions are valued.

For more information about Kregel Publications, visit our web site at www.kregel.com.

Cover and book design: Frank Gutbrod
Cover photo: Doug Menuez, ©PhotoDisc Inc.

Library of Congress Cataloging-in-Publication Data
Ryrie, Caldwell Charles.
  Nailing down a board: serving effectively on the not-for-profit board / Charles C. Ryrie.
      p.   cm.
1. Nonprofit organizations—Management. 2. Directors of corporations. 3. Boards of directors. I. Title.
HD62.6.R96   1999   658.'22—dc21   98-50471
                                                        CIP

ISBN 0-8254-3649-4

Printed in the United States of America

1 2 3 4 5 / 03 02 01 00 99

On the basis of almost thirty years of providing legal services for nonprofit organizations, including churches, I heartily recommend this much needed book to all who serve on such boards. To heed its recommendations cannot help making boards what they ought to be.

J. Shelby Sharpe
Attorney-at-law, Ft. Worth, Texas

As a business man who has also served on the boards of several charitable foundations, I know how important the guidelines contained in this book are in order to make boards as effective as possible.

Robert N. Crawford, President
The Shepherd's Foundation, Dallas, Texas

Contents

Preface

It is required of board members who have been given a trust that they prove faithful. . . .

(an application of 1 Corinthians 4:2)

This booklet focuses on nonprofit boards, including church boards. It has been said that boards seem to have one thing in common—they do not function well, or when they do function, it is at a low percentage of their potential. Though some of the ideas herein come from profit boards, they are applicable to profits and nonprofits alike. The target audience includes everyone who currently serves on a Christian board and those who are being approached to serve. For whatever reasons, nonprofit boards are proliferating today (see end of chapter 1). Many ministries that formerly were functions of churches are now separate nonprofit, tax-exempt entities governed by independent boards. There seem to be more charitable foundations today because people have discovered you do not need to be a Rockefeller to establish one. Large or small, all these organizations need boards.

1

Why This Book?
Who Should Read It?
Why Am I Qualified
to Write It?

During a short break in a board meeting I was attending some years ago, one of the other board members turned to me and asked what I did to relieve the boredom of that meeting. Mind you, this was an annual meeting and one would expect that a number of important matters would be up for serious discussion. But it was boring—no question about it. I don't recall my reply, but I recall his. He said that, since he was a pastor, he was spending the time memorizing the middle verses of hymns!

What a travesty. An annual meeting of an important Christian organization that was so boring that one board member could turn his mind to some other activity and still be aware of what was going on in the meeting (others, like myself, were just daydreaming). That incident raises a number of questions that ought to be addressed both by and about boards.

Some Questions
1. Should boards meet only once a year? Or more often?

2. What items properly belong on an agenda? Since that particular meeting I referred to was an all-day meeting, does its length indicate that the agenda was not carefully focused and targeted on issues that rightly belong to the board, or was it overloaded with matters that should have been handled by others?

3. Whose responsibility is it to keep a meeting moving so that there is no time to memorize the middle verses of hymns? And how is that accomplished (i.e., moving the meeting along, not memorizing verses!)?

4. I should tell you that the pastor I mentioned traveled quite a distance to attend the meeting. Is it more desirable to have members come from anywhere in the country or should the members (or most of them) come from the area in which the organization is headquartered?

These questions and others often are not even given serious consideration, let alone thoroughly discussed, answered, and solutions implemented. To ignore them will likely result in a board rocking along in its usual way (translation: usual rut).

Learning About Boardmanship

If a new board member, trustee, elder, or deacon feels uncomfortable or uninformed about what is expected, he or she should bone up on the subject of board-manship, preferably before beginning to serve on a board. In reality, however, most board members are educated in boardmanship simply and only by serving on boards, learning by trial and error, and thinking themselves experts by virtue of longevity or variety of experience (regardless of what kinds of experience they had during that time).

I vividly recall the fog I was in when I began to serve on boards. With the first boards the fog was caused by inexperience and ignorance. Why was I asked to serve instead of others who were more qualified? What was expected of me? What kinds of questions are appropriate to ask in meetings? And what kind are inappropriate? How will I relate to other board members? Will I mesh with the president or chief executive officer or pastor or leader of the organization?

Even with some board experience under my belt, the fog was not dispelled. Indeed, new fog banks rolled over me as new questions arose. When the founder of an organization is still active and in most cases also serves as chair of the board, how does one relate to him or her, respecting his or her ministry, sacrifice, and dedication, and yet try to guide the chair and the organization in better directions? What is the best process for choosing a new leader? And a very important question that all boards face: What is a truly biblical philosophy of fund raising? The importance of the board being held accountable came increasingly to the forefront of my thinking. These are some of the matters that shall be discussed in this book, and it is hoped the fog will clear so readers and board members may be more effective throughout their service, and so that even good boards may become better ones.

For the most part readers of this book will be associated with nonprofit boards—churches, parachurch organizations, and charitable foundations. But some Christians may be serving on business boards. Regardless of the kind of board—Christian or secular—readers are associated with, certain basic principles of boardmanship apply to all boards. Indeed, we can often learn from non-Christians about boardmanship.

Am I Qualified?

Why am I qualified to write this book? In my own board experiences I've often pondered these questions, and I have been prompted to read some of the books about serving on boards. Then in recent months I have felt a burden to help others from my own board experience (which is drawing to a close), and I felt writing this book might serve that purpose. In preparing to do so, I have read quite a few additional, and more recent, books on both nonprofit and for-profit boards. Like many books on any given subject, some have been very stimulating and helpful and others less so, at least in connection with the purposes of this book.

But my education has not been from books only. During my lifetime I have served on five business boards (for a manufacturing business, a bank, a mutual fund, a food business, and a condominium association); six boards of Christian ministries (a foreign mission board, two youth ministries—one small and the other world-wide—a facility for people with disabilities, a college, and an international ministry to children), three of which were headed by their founders during the time I served; and three charitable foundations (one of which was connected with one of the businesses, the other two being independent).

As you can imagine, these boards provided a wide variety of experiences and challenges. In these board relationships I have been linked with some outstanding board members and CEOs who knew and practiced their boardmanship so very well and whose examples taught me much. Although I have never served on a governing board for a church, I have closely observed such boards of Bible, Presbyterian, and Baptist churches, and I have been called on to help write church constitutions, doctrinal statements, and to advise concerning problems that have arisen within church boards. Generally I made a policy not to serve on Boards of Reference though I have made two exceptions during my life. More about Boards of Reference later in the book.

I have felt an increasing urge to undertake this project in order to help those who are entrusted with board responsibilities make both their own service and that of the board's even better. Close friends who have board experience—both secular and Christian—and with whom I have consulted have urged me to proceed.

Discussing this subject involves opinions that cannot always be proved. But the many books on this subject do not agree even on some of the major points of boardmanship, so readers may disagree with some of my opinions and conclusions. But differences of opinion often help open our minds to ways to do the job better, so it will be worth the time and effort to carefully consider these ideas.

A handbook on boardmanship is particularly timely because of the proliferation of parachurch organizations. These new organizations need boards who know their responsibilities and how to fulfill them. A little historical perspective demonstrates this trend toward increasing numbers of organizations. The Navigators began in 1943. Youth for Christ started in 1945, and Young Life about the same time. Campus Crusade for Christ began in 1951. In 1996 *Christianity Today* highlighted their list of fifty "Up and Comers" in the United States. I made a statistical breakdown of those fifty individuals. Five were associated with educational institutions; ten or so I placed in a miscellaneous category (like a Congressman and editors); nine were identified with a local church and its ministry; twenty-six were associated with or had started their own parachurch organizations.

This list of fifty did not include, for example, people associated with radio and TV ministries, new churches, or Christian schools, which are often independent organizations with their own boards. One concludes that the need for efficient boards is greater today simply because there are more organizations. Many of the ideals and ideas in this book, however, apply equally well to groups other than boards. I wish that some of these procedures had been practiced in the innumerable faculty and committee meetings I have attended! With the time saved, there's no telling what else I might have been able to do!

As I reread these chapters, some of the material sounds like the editorial page of the newspaper—full of opinions as to how to make everything better! I expect that if some things in this book prick the conscience of some boards or board members, there will be the temptation to write off suggestions as "not applicable to our board." Or to say, "Our situation is different, so these principles don't apply to us, though they may be good for others!" And, of course, not everything will be equally helpful to all; size, purposes, and amount of supervision needed will differ among boards. But there are some basic similarities among boards simply because all are boards. So no board should think of itself as so different or special as to ignore what others consider good boardmanship.

I only wish that fifty years ago, when I was elected to my first board, I had known the things outlined in this book!

2

Why Boards at All?

D o we really need boards? Don't they just complicate what otherwise would be simple and straightforward procedures? Can't the Lord lead directly without a board, especially if the organization is small?

Isn't church government a democracy? Why then should elders and/or deacons come between Christ the Head of the church and the members of His body? Won't boards sometimes tend to stifle the leading of the Holy Spirit? Even if questions like these aren't asked out loud, they sometimes go through our minds.

There are at least *three* biblical justifications for boards or board-like entities in organizations.

The Example of the New Testament
The *first* justification stands on the clear biblical teaching concerning the need for elders and deacons in the organizational structure of local churches. A local

church as pictured in the New Testament is not simply any group that happens to meet together on occasion. New Testament churches were organized groups. However an organization may label its governing group— elders, deacons, stewards, bishops—they will have such a group or groups in its organizational structure. Furthermore, organization was deemed necessary when churches began, not just later after they had been functioning for some time (see Acts 14:23).

The very first organization took place not long after the church began on the Day of Pentecost. Of the thousands who were saved on the Day of Pentecost, undoubtedly a number went back to their various homes elsewhere in the Roman empire. But many stayed on to be instructed in their newfound faith. For this reason lands and houses were sold so money would be available to supply the needs of those who temporarily remained in Jerusalem.

But even after they returned to their homes another need arose, that of the support of widows in Judea. In Judaism there existed a fund that was used to support Jewish widows (2 Macc. 3:10). But when a number of them became Christians that support was cut off. So the church made itself responsible for those widows. Some were Greek-speaking Jewish Christian widows and others were Aramaic-speaking Jewish Christian widows. The former group felt that they were not being supported to the same extent that the latter group was. So a dispute arose, and the apostles solved the problem by having seven men selected to "serve tables" (Acts 6:5).

Customarily these seven are called deacons (from the word *serve*). From the text it is clear that the apostles were the primary "board of directors" and the seven deacons were a subsidiary part of the early organization of the believers in Jerusalem. Notice something about the apostles and the deacons that will keep coming up in this book: both groups knew what their particular mission was and kept that mission in clear focus, undiluted and undiverted as they carried it out. The apostles' mission was to pray and minister the Word. The deacons' was to care for the widows. Each group "stuck to its guns."

The first mention of elders in relation to the New Testament church is in Acts 11:30 and refers to the recognized official group who received the famine relief money sent to Jerusalem. This would have occurred around A.D. 46. Elders formed the governing councils of synagogues both in Palestine and elsewhere (Luke 7:3), so it was not unexpected that the early church carried elders over into their organizational structure. Eventually deacons, too, became a recognized group of leaders along with elders in New Testament churches (Phil. 1:1).

On his first missionary trip into parts of Asia Minor (A.D. 47–48), Paul saw many people converted and joined together into churches in various places: Antioch (in Pisidia), Derbe, Lystra, and Iconium being mentioned in particular. On the return leg of that first journey Paul revisited those churches to strengthen and encourage the new believers and to appoint elders "in every church" (Acts 14:23). Only a few months—perhaps only weeks—would have passed between the time of the assembling of new converts into local churches and Paul's appointing elders for them. Paul obviously considered organization necessary for the proper functioning of those churches he had established. He did not leave them without human leadership.

So one significant reason for having boards is the example of organization in the New Testament churches.

The Wisdom of the Proverbs

Several proverbs clearly give a *second* reason why boards are necessary. One says, "Where there is no guidance the people fall, But in abundance of counselors there is victory" (Prov. 11:14). The word "guidance" relates to the handling and steering of a ship. Again: "Without consultation, plans are frustrated, But with many counselors they succeed" (15:22). And again: "Prepare plans by consultation, And make war by wise guidance" (20:18). And yet again: "For by wise guidance you will wage war, And in abundance of counselors there is victory" (24:6). In a similar vein Proverbs 24:3–4 (as paraphrased vividly in The Living Bible) declares: "Any enterprise is built by wise planning, becomes strong through common sense, and profits wonderfully by keeping abreast of the facts." Any one or all of these proverbs might well be framed and hung in the boardrooms of America.

While it is true that one can hear advice from too many people, these proverbs clearly underscore the necessity of listening to others and not shutting out their counsel even if they do not always agree. Effective boards can and should follow the wisdom of these proverbs.

The Necessity for Accountability

A *third* reason for needing boards is that they provide
for accountability. To be sure, some boards are so inbred with family members and close friends that issues
of accountability are seldom if ever raised. Cronyism
("partiality to cronies . . . appointment of . . . hangers-
on without regard to their qualifications") must never
be allowed to eclipse the fiduciary and mission responsibilities of a board. Such responsibilities include, but
certainly are not limited to, the philosophy of fund raising, the use of funds, the honesty and integrity of reports
to constituencies, decisions based on full and free
discussion in meetings, nothing ever done "under the
table" or by one or two members, periodic review and
evaluations of personnel and programs, and total integrity in all actions and activities.

The apostle Paul furnishes a fine biblical example of
sensitivity to accountability. You remember that at one
time in his ministry he was involved in collecting
money for the impoverished believers in Jerusalem.
He had been spearheading this effort for several years
(2 Cor. 9:2; Gal. 2:10), but gifts from the Corinthians
had fallen behind. Other churches, like those in
Philippi, Thessalonica, and Berea, had contributed even
though they were in financial straits (2 Cor. 8:1–6). Paul
holds them up as good examples for the Corinthians
to follow.

But it is Paul's handling of the money that shows his
sensitivity to accountability. He himself did not handle
it, but delegated the matter to three "trustees." Titus
was one (2 Cor. 8:18a); an unnamed but well-known
and highly respected brother whom the churches chose

was the second (v. 18b); and a third was another brother, also unnamed, but one who had been fully tested and found diligent in many things (v. 22). These "trustees," though well-known to and approved by Paul, were not selected by him (Titus had volunteered and the other two were chosen by the churches). They would serve to forestall any suspicions or innuendoes being whispered about Paul that he was personally profiting in some way from this collection, and they would see to it that everything was done openly and above board.

Such integrity is mandatory for all boards, certainly for Christian ones. And there cannot be integrity without full and regular accountability.

So there are three reasons that boards are desirable—the example of the organization of the churches, the wisdom gained by having counselors, and the need for accountability, which ultimately rests in the board.

If these reasons are not sufficient, then remember that governmental laws usually require recognized organizations to have a board!

3

How to Choose Board Members

C hoosing board members must be done with the utmost care. Fortunately, there are guidelines that can improve the selection process.

For a New Work

When a ministry is just being established, the board will likely be small and composed of family and/or friends of the founder. There is nothing inherently wrong with this, unless board appointments continue in the same pattern as the work grows. A growing work requires that the number of family members be diminished, lest the board become too inbred and the family in reality makes all the decisions, the non-family members simply agreeing. At the beginning, three board members may be all that are needed, but as a work grows, the board will also need to grow, but not too much. Boards should be very cautious about enlarging themselves to the point of gridlock or rubber-stamping—gridlock because there cannot be full and free discussion if the group is too large, and rubber-stamping because members are reluctant to differ or prolong a meeting.

For a Church

Church boards are chosen in different ways. In all cases, however, the leaders (whether called elders, stewards, deacons, deaconesses, bishops) must be biblically qualified according to 1 Timothy 3:1–13 and Titus 1:5–9. Qualified elders and deacons must be men, for one of the qualifications is "husband of one wife"— hardly possible for a woman.

There were women who served (the general meaning of deacon and deaconess) in New Testament times (Rom. 16:1), but whether there was a recognized group of "deaconesses" in New Testament days is unclear. Certainly by the fourth century there was such an officially recognized group of deaconesses. Whether the women mentioned in 1 Timothy 3:11 were deaconesses or the wives of deacons is also debated, but their qualifications, whichever they were, are clearly described in that verse. If a church has officially recognized deaconesses, they need to meet the qualifications in that verse.

Those Scriptures list qualifications clearly. The interpretation of some of them is debated, and the local church may have to make policy decisions about its

understanding and application of those verses that are
debated, and then follow those policies when choosing its leaders. This book does not discuss those
qualifications about which there is debate.

But how to choose leaders is not so clearly explained.
In the case of the first helpers of the apostles, the believers were to "look over" the people (Acts 6:3—the
same word as bishop, an overseer) and bring their
choices to the apostles, who actually appointed them
(the same word as used in Titus 1:5 of Titus's appointing elders). One might say the group nominated, and
the apostles appointed.

Paul himself directly appointed elders in the new
churches established on his first missionary trip (Acts
14:23). Paul also designated Titus to appoint elders in
the churches in Crete (Titus 1:5). What the procedure
was after the apostles passed off the scene, the Scripture does not say. The kind of church government a
congregation has usually is what determines the procedure used today. In a hierarchical government, leaders will be appointed. In the federal pattern they will
likely be chosen by the existing elders. In congrega-
tionalism they will be elected by the members. Many
churches use a combination of methods; for example,
the elders nominate the candidates, and the members
vote on them.

It goes without saying (or does it?) that if a church
has a doctrinal statement, the leadership must not only
agree to it with their whole hearts and minds, they
must support and teach it. It is wrong for a leader to
say publicly that he or she will support a doctrinal

position while disagreeing with it privately. Or to say he or she does not agree with some part or parts, but in public will not contradict or question these areas. Just keeping silence often raises doubts in the minds of others.

I have been involved in interviewing, recommending, and sometimes actually hiring prospective faculty in three different schools, and I would never vote for someone who doubted or disagreed with some part of the doctrinal position but who tried to give assurance that he or she would not make an issue of that matter in the classroom. Not making an issue inevitably makes an issue, for it raises questions about that issue in the minds of students. I have seen schools regret hiring someone under those conditions.

For an Established and Ongoing Work

If a board is to be effective, then nothing can be more important than choosing the right members. In an ongoing work, vacancies inevitably occur, either because of resignation, retirement, or death. Resignation may result from a number of reasons—ill health, differences of opinion with the purpose of the organization and/or its CEO, or some new interest taking precedence. For whatever reasons, vacancies will occur, and a board should have in place guidelines for finding and electing those who meet qualifications for association with and governance of that ministry.

General Guidelines

General and timeless guidelines include these.

1. The selection process should include the entire board. Along the way a committee may do some of the work, but the whole board should be informed and included at each step of the process. It is a mistake to allow one or two forceful members to control the process and ramrod their choice(s) through the board. Even the CEO (including a pastor) should be careful not to control the selection process in order to bring on board those who either are the CEO's friends or who can be counted on to share his or her viewpoints.

This temptation seems to be especially strong in the case of a new CEO who is likely to consider his existing board to be dragging their collective feet in promoting all the wonderful new ideas he or she has for the organization. Therefore, the CEO pushes for new members who will be favorable to his or her plans and, like President Franklin Roosevelt, who tried to pack the Supreme Court by enlarging it with his own nominees, "packs" the board with his or her choices, who may in many cases be unknown to the existing board members. The board must not acquiesce to that kind of pressure.

I was in one board meeting when a new board member was introduced for the first time to the majority of the members and elected at that same meeting. He was the choice of one of the members, and even the chair scarcely could recall his name when he introduced him. If a new CEO comes on board, one of his or her top priorities is to get to know the existing board, and doubtless he or she will discover some treasures that do not need to be replaced or diluted by the CEO's choice of new members.

2. Board members should always be on the lookout for possible new members, whether or not any are needed at a given time. Then when the time comes to nominate new members, potential candidates will have been observed for some time by existing members before being considered by the whole board.

When I served on another board, I thought of an acquaintance who I thought would fit that board and its work well. The time came when a vacancy did occur, and in the initial discussions another member suggested that man's name without any previous discussion between the two of us. That we both had been thinking independently for some time of this man encouraged the board to consider him seriously. Of course, everyone on a board should be made to feel free to suggest potential candidates for membership and to discuss those who are suggested.

3. Pray individually and as a group for the Lord's leading in the choice(s) to be made. As well as we can know other individuals, God knows all of us better than we know either ourselves or others. Too, He alone knows the future and what will be needed in the life of an organization as well as who will be best suited to meet those yet unforeseen needs. This is not to say that a board should not use its best judgment in evaluating a candidate, but it is to say that there may be times when the best judgment may not produce the best choice. But prayer will. With all the procedures a board may use, there must be an overriding conviction from the Lord that this person is His choice.

4. Pursue only one potential candidate at a time. Do not interview several and then decide among them. This is not an election of one from among several, but a selection or rejection of only one at a time.

Specific Guidelines

Some specific guidelines for the selection process include the following.

1. After the entire board has discussed possible candidates, two or three members or the nominating committee should sit down with the prospective candidate in an informal, comfortable setting and talk about the organization, about the candidate, and about a possible relationship. This is not a cross-examination but a get-acquainted meeting for both parties. Both should understand that for any reason, expressed or unexpressed, either party may decide not to go further with the matter. During this conversation(s) everything should be placed out in the open and discussed freely and frankly. Such matters as compatibility with the mission and doctrinal stand of the organization, lifestyle matters that are important to the ministry, what participation is expected of a board member, the need for keeping confidences without exception, and the time required are areas that can well be discussed at this preliminary stage. In addition, the board members will want to provide the potential candidate with any materials that would not breech confidentiality but that would help acquaint the person with the structure and function of the board.

Once when I was being considered for membership on a board, I asked to see a copy of the constitution and bylaws of the organization. This was an appropriate request, for to examine those documents would breech no confidences. But not only had the chair not brought them with him, he also told me he wasn't sure where copies were, but he would look into it! That experience happened early on in my life, so when later I was involved in interviewing prospective members I made sure they were provided with appropriate documents.

The necessity for compatibility of lifestyle on the part of the board and workers in an organization needs to be given high priority when choosing board members. It is unrealistic to expect missionaries, for example, to exhibit a particular lifestyle when they see their leaders (board members) not conforming to the same standards. It ought also to be embarrassing to the board if a member or members do not exhibit agreed upon standards. And the board members involved ought to be not only willing but happy to conform, even if it means restricting what they consider to be their liberty, for the sake of having a ministry on that board and to that organization.

2. The individuals who did the interviewing then bring back a report to the entire board. The report should include discrete inquiries made to someone outside the board as to the suitability of the prospect. This could be done before the initial interview or at this point. But if inquiries are made, they must be handled very delicately. If, for example, the prospect serves on another board and someone on that board is

known to someone on the board doing the interviewing, then it might be possible to make a discrete
inquiry that would help in making a decision about
the prospect. For certain, inquiry should be made as
to the prospect's involvement in his or her local church.
After discussion and lots of prayer and taking plenty
of time for both, then a decision can be made. If there
is doubt, it is better not to proceed even if a vacancy
goes unfilled for some time.

3. If everything is Go, then the board proceeds to
elect the person. But the prospect should not be present
during the meeting at which he or she is elected nor
be kept waiting in the wings to come in after the election. Election at one meeting; first attendance for the
new member at the following meeting.

Other guidelines may be needed by organizations that
have special requirements. But in general the above
guidelines will guard and guide the selection process.

4

How *Not* to Choose Board Members

J ust as there are guidelines for choosing effective board members, there are also some caveats. They won't apply in all cases; nevertheless, too often these caveats are ignored in the interests of expediency or other inappropriate reasons.

Don't Be in a Hurry

It takes lots of patience and prayer and perception to develop a good board. Vacancies do not have to be filled as soon as they occur or even soon after. Sometimes they do not need to be filled at all. In my opinion boards are usually too large (more of that later). When, however, it is determined that a vacancy needs to be filled, proceed deliberately. It may be that the board has had some candidates "in the wings," in which case the process of choosing someone has a head start. But if the board is starting from scratch, then by all means don't be in a hurry. Once a person is elected, it is not easy to remove him or her.

Neither be in such a hurry that the becoming acquainted/ investigative process is cut short. "Oh, we know the person well. There's no need to talk with him except to find out if he is willing to serve. Let's save time and go ahead and ask him." That's a serious mistake. Or sometimes the rest of the board will simply go along with a member who is championing the candidate and who attests to knowing the person very well.

This happened on a board of a Christian ministry on which I once served. One of the officers of the board proposed a person with whom he had served for some time on their church board. As I remember, the candidate was chair of that church board. So rather than going through the customary process of having several visits with the man, we simply voted to ask him to join the board. In due time it came to light that he had a practice that would not be acceptable to the board and the constituents the organization served. What to do? Well, I was drafted to go to the man and seek his resignation. He was very understanding and cooperative. All was well that ended well, though it was embarrassing and awkward for a time. And it could have been avoided if a short cut had not been taken.

Don't Necessarily Look for "Important" People
Too often board members are chosen because they are well known either in the Christian or the business community. This assumes that having a recognized name listed on the board lends some special credence

to the organization. It may do that, but the person may be so important that he or she does not have time to do much more than lend his or her name to the organization. If that is the case, then ask the person to serve on a Board of Reference on which he or she is not expected to do anything more than lend a famous name.

"Importance" is often equated with wealth. So certain people are often chosen as board members because they can personally give as well as attract money to the organization. One writer summarized it this way: It used to be that a board member provided work, wealth, and wisdom to the board; but now it's give, get, or get off![1] Unquestionably board members should give to the organizations they govern. If they do not give at all or merely give token gifts, then they should resign, for "where your treasure is, there will your heart be also" (Matt. 6:21). If they give none or little of their treasure, then it's a sure sign that they are giving none or little of their hearts to their respective groups.

I once had a sharp disagreement with a fellow board member who was defending another board member (who was also his close friend) for not giving even one dollar for several years to the organization. His defense was that board members were not chosen for what they could give. With that I wholeheartedly agreed, but I also insisted that the man could surely give at least $50 a year (actually he could have given much more). My fellow board member was making a very valid and often overlooked point—you do not choose board members simply because they are wealthy. But I was also making a valid point—you can expect them regularly to give something to the organization.

A stronger view was represented in an interview that Peter Drucker conducted with a former president of Fuller Seminary. In response to the matter of recruiting trustees, the president said the following.

> We say to them: "We expect you to give proportionate to your means, and in your giving to assign a high priority to our institution. Your local church and perhaps one other organization can be as important to you as Fuller, but we don't want Fuller to be any lower than third, and we would prefer Fuller to be second behind the commitment to the local church." I also will talk to them about including Fuller as part of their estate, because ultimately with trustees you not only want year-by-year contributions. You want to participate in some form or another, through trusts or annuities or wills, in the final distribution of their wealth."[2]

Incidentally (or is it?), Fuller Seminary in 1996 had forty-three members on its board.

Do not misunderstand. I am neither endorsing nor discouraging the inclusion of wealthy people on boards or as elders and trustees. I am only emphasizing that a godly life, Bible knowledge (so as to have biblical perspectives), spiritual maturity, and discernment are primary qualifications. Whether or not the person has a lot or money is of much less importance.

Don't Assume That Because a Person Runs a Business Well, He or She Can Run the Lord's Work Well

One may or may not be able to do so. For example, one's business may require the regular borrowing of money. Will such experience allow that person to face objectively the question whether or not a Christian work should borrow money, and if so, under what circumstances? If not, why not? Or another example. Should outplacing (translation: firing) practices used by businesses be carried over unchanged into a Christian work? Or how is one's testimony affected by not paying bills on time, a procedure businesses sometimes do deliberately in order to take advantage of the "float." Christian organizations sometimes do it because they have not planned well.

Of course, there are Christian businessmen and women who conduct their businesses on Christian principles and whose experiences can be of immense value to a Christian organization. Blessed is the board whose membership includes such people.

Don't Seek Someone Who Is Already Heavily Involved in Other Ministries

The only uniform exception to this principle is involvement in one's local church. In addition to that involvement, it is hoped that the member would limit his or her leadership involvement to one or two other organizations. The ideal is three or four board responsibilities at most. A board must expect intelligent and active involvement in its affairs; spreading oneself too thin will inevitably diminish such participation.

I have personally known one exception to this. After retiring from an investment business, this person devoted himself to being a professional board member; i.e., all he did was serve on boards. His particular business experience had exposed him to a variety of enterprises, which gave him the ability to serve on a variety of boards. And having served with him on one of the business boards, I can testify that his involvement was never less than it should have been. Indeed, the variety of his board service brought to the boards on which he served many helpful insights, yet he never divulged anything confidential.

Don't Look for Professionals So That They Can Do Work for the Group (Hopefully Gratis!)

More than once have I heard in a board meeting that "we need a lawyer [or a CPA or a doctor] on this board"; meaning, of course, "Then we can have him provide his professional expertise as a free service to the organization." Doing work for the organization and being consulted for advice by the organization are two different things. If a board includes an attorney, there is every reason for the CEO or the board to consult him or her for advice on legal matters, assuming the attorney is qualified in the area consulted upon. But to have an attorney board member do the legal work of the organization is not only unwise but may involve a conflict of interest. Especially if the attorney does such work for a lower than customary charge or for none at all. Such a situation places the board in a position where they cannot demand accountability from the member who provides the service. Or worse, the board cannot easily fire the person while he or she remains a member of the board. Consultation should be done without charge, but work should be paid for and preferably done by someone who is not a member of the board.

Don't Go Too Far Afield Geographically in Assembling a Board

Because of technological advances, this suggestion may be of less importance today than it was a generation ago. Nevertheless, a board whose membership is widely scattered will likely meet only three or four times a year, simply because of the time and expense involved in travel. Even an executive committee composed of local members does not fully overcome this obstacle. A more local board, however, can meet more frequently and can also have social contact and fellowship that is not possible when the members are scattered. I have served on boards that met (1) annually, (2) on call (which meant very seldom), (3) four times a year, (4) every other month, and (5) monthly. Members tend to prefer fewer meetings, but such does not always benefit the organization. To be sure, monthly and even bimonthly meetings come around quickly enough, but the responsibility of oversight is more carefully discharged and the agendas for those meetings less cluttered. Too, the CEO can keep in closer touch with individual members when they are nearby and can meet for breakfast or lunch conveniently.

Teleconferencing is no substitute for face-to-face meetings. You can't see body language over the telephone. Neither is there as much free discussion. Phone conferences may be suitable for very routine matters that do not require discussion, or they may suit a very small board, since a board of three, say, can probably discuss as freely over the phone as they could in person.

Don't Overload a Board with Too Many Members

Christian ministries often tend to have too large boards, unless the organization is new and a family or a few close associates have founded the ministry. But as organizations mature, they tend to enlarge their boards to the point that (1) either the board is a rubber stamp, (2) a few strong members lead and control the board, or (3) an executive committee becomes the de facto board. A reasonably sized board can more easily have full and free discussions, can employ the abilities of all its members, and can mold itself into a cohesive unit more readily.

A ten-member board directs the giant Exxon Corporation. The same number directs AT&T. An eleven-member board runs IBM. NCR manages with eight. But a leading Christian publishing organization has a twenty-six-member board; a Bible institute, eighteen; a Christian college, thirty-four; and a sports ministry, twenty-five. I checked six conservative seminaries and the number of their board members was twenty-three, twenty-seven, thirty, thirty-one, forty-three, and fifty-one. The prize, however, goes to a large hospital's charitable foundation, which has eighty-nine! Doubtless this large number is not for governance but for fund raising, for the list includes the wealthy of the area. The average number of board members for independent colleges is thirty-two.[3] In my judgment, however, that large average number does not justify having such large boards.

Elder boards of churches seem to have nine to twelve members, although a pastor friend of mine recently told me his church only had five. I asked him how he liked having such a small board of elders. His response was that small is best because meetings were more open and useful, and he could also minister personally to five much better than if the board were larger. Deacon bodies are often even larger, especially in denominations that ordain deacons for life. Some large churches have hundreds of deacons. Even though deacons may rotate off and on the board again and again, the number is much too large to function as a board should. The members of such large church boards function more as sounding than governing boards. It is beyond me why large boards are needed, regardless of the kind of organization they direct. Indeed, I think a large number of members hinders board work. The best functioning boards on which I have served had five to seven members.

I find myself in agreement with John Carver who wrote, "With respect to board size, the simple rule is to justify any number over seven. There is nothing magic about the number seven; however, as boards grow progressively beyond this size, they pay an increasingly higher price in awkwardness, discipline, and unfocused energy. . . . Large boards are easier to manipulate.

Members of large groups tend to assume less responsibility as individuals. Large boards have more difficulty setting meeting dates, deliberating issues, and staying on task."[4]

Don't Have Board Members
Whose Lifestyle Differs from the Constituency's

One cannot expect the constituency of an organization to give its confidence and support to a ministry whose board members have different (translation: looser) standards for Christian living. I once asked the president of a Christian school whether or not the students, staff, faculty, and board were allowed to consume alcoholic beverages. His answer was that the students, faculty, and staff could not but the board could. His rationale was that the board members were volunteering their time freely and therefore could not be asked to conform to restrictive standards. Whether or not that is a justifiable reason, it clearly does not provide a good example. By that same logic, those board members should not be expected to meet attendance requirements or serve on committees since they are volunteers. The lifestyles of both the Old Testament priests and the New Testament elders and deacons were more restricted than those of others (Lev. 10:9–11; 21:1–24; 1 Tim. 3:1–13; Titus 1:5–9). The lifestyles of our board leaders should be no less.

Of course, we do not live in an ideal world, and no board can be ideal. But it's one thing to have and keep high standards in mind even though you cannot always meet them, and it is quite a different matter to adjust or lower the standards in order to accommodate situations or to meet expediencies.

5

Before You Say "Yes"

So you have been approached by your church or another organization to join their board. Before flattery takes over and you agree to do so, there are some questions you should ask—some you ask of yourself; some you ask of others even if you think you know the work well. If you do agree to serve you will be entering a new relationship with the group even though you might have previously had close contact with it.

Materials You Need to Have in Hand

Presumably during preliminary contacts with people in the organization, you will have received some of the basic materials concerning the group. Certainly they would include articles of incorporation, by-laws, purpose statements, governing structure and personnel, audited financial statements, publicity and fund raising materials, and perhaps a history of the ministry. Even churches should provide such material. Having this information in hand will give you opportunity to

investigate and consider the ministry more objectively
and without outside pressure.

Questions to Ask Yourself

Perhaps the most crucial question is whether you
wholeheartedly believe in the mission and purpose of
the ministry. If you have reservations, then someone
else may better serve the group. Try to distinguish between the mission or purpose of the organization and
the programs it has. In this way you will be able to focus
more clearly on the degree of support you can give to
the mission *per se*. Then you can move from mission
to programs and assess whether the programs are in
accord with that mission. If you feel it necessary, ask to
visit some of the activities of the ministry so you can
personally see and become better acquainted with what
the group does. If that is not possible—for instance, in
relation to a foreign mission board—then read a number
of reports and prayer letters from the members of the
mission. To conclude that there could be programs that
would better carry out the mission does not in itself
preclude your serving on the board. Indeed, you will be
a better board member for having investigated these
things ahead of time.

Another important consideration is whether you can
afford the time to be an effective board member. Only
you and your family can answer that question, and
your family should have input to the discussion. It is
not fair to the organization if you serve knowing you
do not have the time, and it is unwise for you to lend
your name to something you cannot monitor closely.

Questions to Ask About Finances

Is there an annual budget? How accurate is it in relation to actual income and expenses? Is it examined and adjusted if necessary during the fiscal year? Does it demonstrate financial stability of the organization? Are bills paid promptly? Is financial information made available to the public? Do you agree with the methods of raising funds? Have you seen samples of fund raising appeals? Are these appeals honest? Do monies received go toward the purposes for which they were designated? Is there an outside audit? Is there anything that raised in the past or might trigger in the future an inquiry or examination by the Internal Revenue Service?

Questions to Ask About Legal Matters

Sometimes charitable groups, including churches, become involved in lawsuits, either as a plaintiff or defendant. You need to know if this has ever happened or if there are any pending legal actions. Too, it is advisable to inquire about any possible conflict of interest any board member may conceivably have. Conflicts of interest often relate to work a board member may contract to do for the organization, which makes the member both an employee of the organization and one of his own bosses at the same time.

Questions to Ask Others

Somewhere during the time of "courtship" of a new board member, there should be opportunity for the prospect to ask questions of current or past members of the board. Current members, however, may be tempted to gloss over existing problems in order to get you to say "yes." Former board members can usually be more frank about problems as well as blessings from their experience on the board. I think this would be especially true in relation to church boards, where the membership changes more frequently and where former leaders are likely to still be involved in the church. Of course, if you suspect a lack of integrity on the part of the organization or its board, then beware and investigate before making a decision.

The Question to Ask Your Heavenly Father

There's just one: Is this Your will for me at this time in my life?

6

Why and How
to Retire Board Members

There comes a time when a board member needs to retire. Some retire voluntarily; others need a nudge. When such time arrives, the board should have in place policies and procedures that can be used uniformly so that everyone is treated fairly and kindly.

Board members retire for a number of reasons: (1) age; (2) loss of interest in the work; (3) poor attendance at meetings; (4) other interests taking priority; (5) term limits (if the board has such) having been reached; or (6) poor results of an evaluation (if the board conducts one).

Age
Should the board have a specific age at which members must retire? Some do and others do not. While it can be argued that a seventy-five-year-old board

member may contribute more and be sharper than a sixty-year-old, it seems best to have a mandatory retirement age. Businesses do—why not Christians organizations also? Age seventy is often suggested in the literature. Some add that a board member may be asked to stay on after seventy on a year-to-year basis, but generally no later than seventy-two or sometimes seventy-five. Nevertheless, there may be good reasons to make exceptions even to a maximum age for serving, but always on a year-to-year, case-by-case basis.

While a valid argument can be made for the continuity and wisdom an older board member contributes, continuing too long in board service prevents the addition of a younger member, unless, of course, the board is enlarged. This is not always the best idea, since to enlarge may simply be the board's way of not facing the need to have someone retire.

If age or infirmity dictates the retirement of a valued and faithful board member, he or she can be moved to an emeritus status or to a board of reference if the organization has one. Emeritus means the individual may hold as an honorary title the same title he or she had while active. An emeritus professor may hold the same title he or she had while serving on a faculty (e.g., professor of English, emeritus); an emeritus board member may be designated as emeritus director of XYZ organization. In contrast, one who simply retires is a former member of the board of directors but not emeritus unless the board bestows that title on him or her. Emeriti directors may certainly be listed in the literature of the organization, but it seems preferable that they not attend meetings, even if they do not vote. Otherwise a strong board member who becomes an emeritus can continue to exert considerable influence if he or she is present at meetings. However, emeriti and their spouses should be encouraged to remain involved in social functions and ceremonies of the board (e.g., installations, commencements, etc.).

Boards of reference can serve two purposes. For a new organization they can give credence to the too-new-to-be-well-known group because of the high profile individuals who allow their names to be listed on a board of reference. For an established organization a board of reference lends additional credibility to the organization as well as provides a continuing relationship for those who have served on the board of directors. Boards of reference need to be kept informed of the activities and plans of the organization. They should be encouraged to offer suggestions, but they do not necessarily have to hold meetings at all. And certainly their personnel should be kept up-to-date. How often I have seen letterheads that list the board of reference, some members of that board having died several years earlier.

Loss of Interest

Though not inevitable, it is not unexpected that a board member may lose interest in the group he or she serves. There may be perfectly good and justifiable circumstances for this happening. Or the member may simply find his or her personal goals or lifestyle differing from that of the organization. If this happens, then the honorable thing to do is to resign quietly. If the mission of the organization is clear and there is no good reason for changing it, yet there are members who want to change it into something radically different, then those people should resign and start their own organization. This is not to say that the mission does not sometimes need to be changed, but it is to say that campaigning to do so on the part of some may lead to dilution, division, or even the demise of the organization. New ways to fulfill the group's mission is one thing; a basic change in the mission is quite another. If some feel a change is necessary, while the majority do not, then let the few resign so as not to ruin the organization.

Poor Attendance

This is a touchy subject many boards do not want to face. Should there be an attendance policy? Yes, of course, there should be. If someone cannot regularly attend, then what good is that person to the ministry? Even the Securities and Exchange Commission requires listing the attendance of board members of public companies in their proxy statements, a 75 percent attendance at meetings each year being the standard. Now, of course, there may be justifiable reasons why someone cannot attend at least for a time (e.g., illness), but exceptions can be made in those cases. Notwithstanding, all things being equal, a board must expect its members to regularly attend its meetings.

A board on which I once served did not have an attendance policy. A couple of members seldom or never showed up, always for what they considered to be good reasons. This went on for two or three years, and we did not know what to do, for these absentee members had served the board well. No one wanted to hurt their feelings or appear to disregard their past contributions. Yet the ministry was not being well served. So several members agreed to approach these folks and lay the problem before them. To their credit, one resigned while the other committed to attend regularly. Then the board did write an attendance policy, which was used as a standard from that time on.

Other Interests Taking Priority

People's interests do change. Therefore it would not be unusual or unexpected that another ministry might attract a board member's interest. Or he or she may simply be growing weary of service on a particular board. Such is not necessarily the fault of the ministry or of the individual. The ministry may still be very much on target, yet the board member is suffering "board burnout." In either case (other interests or burnout), the individual should simply close that board chapter of his or her life whether or not that member ever takes on other board memberships. A departure can be done with understanding and good feeling on everyone's part, particularly if all sense that this is the will of God. God certainly can lead to ending a healthy board relationship, and a separation may have the good result of filling that vacancy with someone who brings a new freshness and zest to the work.

A Red Flag

For some, retirement is often traumatic, even when it comes for good and understandable reasons. When retirement of a board member becomes necessary for whatever reason, it should be handled with love, gentleness, and consideration for his or her feelings. Some sort of public recognition is certainly appropriate, especially when the member has served faithfully for many years. And there may even be cases where it is more Christlike to allow the individual to stay on the board—even though he or she contributes little outwardly—rather than enforcing a retirement age or moving that person to a board of reference. By prayer and support of that ministry, he or she may be contributing much that is not seen. Let the board member stay and come to meetings. His or her very presence, like that of the venerable patriarchs, will clothe the entire board with his or her mantle of blessing.

Guidelines for retiring a board member should be in place and not made up as the board goes along. We all need to have an understanding of the ideal, but we cannot always meet the ideal, nor is it always necessary to force ourselves to do so. Policies can be changed, and exceptions can be made. A board will always in all matters, including retirements, have to be sensitive to the Lord's leading and be kind one to another.

7

Primary Responsibilities of a Board

Although written about for-profit boards, the following advises what a board does *not* do, and it applies equally well to nonprofits.

> *We* [the board] *don't manage the company.* This is a rule that the rest of the world finds difficult to understand. After all, the board is always shown at the top of the organization chart. But a moment's thought should convince anyone that a group of individuals who get together every month or two cannot be seriously regarded as managing the company. We govern; the executives manage.

> *We don't set strategy....* if the board were to set strategy it would, in the process, give away its power and responsibility for questioning and evaluating strategy alternatives.[1]

In their order of importance, I would list the responsibilities of a board as follows.

1. Defining the mission of the organization (even a church needs to do this, and more so these days when churches seem to be into many programs that may or may not be related to its mission).

2. Choosing and caring for the CEO (or pastor in the case of a church).

3. Periodically reviewing and evaluating the performance of both the board and the CEO.

4. Setting policies (before they are needed!) for a number of functions, especially in relation to financial matters and necessary committees.

The Mission Statement

A mission statement for the organization should be clear, concise, and sharply focused. It may change now and again, but always the changes should be clear, concise, and sharply focused so that the board understands clearly the goals of the organization. The mission statement should always be kept in the forefront of the board's thinking to guide the implementation of the mission and to guard from deviating from it, regardless of how worthy deviations might seem to be.

A clear mission statement is also necessary for effective evaluation of both the CEO and the board. A fuzzy or forgotten statement will cause the board to evaluate the methods being used rather than whether or not the goals are being attained. Asking the question, Are we doing what our stated mission requires? will go a long way in correctly determining the methods necessary to accomplish those goals. Then others, not the board, implement the strategy.

Failure to have and to implement a clearly defined mission leads the board to constantly evaluate its methods (e.g., how many meetings should we have, how many committees, etc.) rather than how well it has attained its goals. Fuzziness must be replaced by focus.

It is probably easier for a nonprofit and/or parachurch organization to define its mission than for a local church to do so. At first glance, just the opposite would seem to be true, but think about it. If you asked the members of almost any evangelical church what is the mission of their church, many of the responses would include similar goals. Most would say, to win the lost and to disciple believers. Well and good, but then the leaders must decide what programs are doing this, which may lead to the conclusion that some programs need to be added, some eliminated, and some perhaps scaled down or expanded.

Some might try to summarize by simply referring to the Great Commission. But is that a complete enough statement? What about the church's responsibilities to worship, to discipline, to care for widows and the poor (none of which is expressed in the Great Commission but are stated elsewhere in the New Testament)? Would these be in a mission statement? If not, why not? If so, then what is being done to implement these responsibilities? What in the mission statement justifies an elaborate (and often expensive) music program? Worship, perhaps. What justifies building a gymnasium? Attracting unsaved, perhaps. Are social and entertainment programs for seniors part of discipling them?

It would be wise for the leaders to evaluate and re-evaluate the worthwhileness of every program in relation to carrying out the mission of that local church. Otherwise the activities of a church will grow like Topsy, diluting and diverting from the purpose of a church. If any activity is a goal of the mission, then it rightly belongs in the mission statement. If any is an implementation of the mission, then it should do just that, clearly and justifiably, which does not necessarily mean elaborately.

For nonprofit organizations, often the founding document submitted to the Internal Revenue Service for approval is very broadly written so that if approved it permits the organization to do many things. But then the mission statement to be formulated should be focused and concise. "The board not only helps think through the institution's mission, it is the guardian of that mission, and makes sure the organization lives up to its basic commitment."[2]

Though writing particularly about bank boards, Don Wright gives a vivid example of contrasting mission statements.[3] Writing about the necessity of clearly defining one's business, he contrasts the old Braniff Airways with the newer Southwest Airlines. Braniff, he says, determined to acquire all the routes it could get, and eventually went bankrupt more than once.

Southwest, on the other hand, began by operating only between the major cities in Texas. Now, of course, it has expanded nationwide, but only when it could handle such expansion and by doing it in deliberate stages.

The downsizing and selling off assets of large corporations in the 80s and 90s was done because corporations realized that they needed to focus on their core businesses and divest themselves of acquisitions they had made in the name of expansion. Quaker Oats' acquisition, failure, and fire sale of Snapple drinks is one example. AT&T's spin off of NCR and Lucent in order to concentrate on its core business furnishes another example. Both of these examples occurred in the mid-90s. Christian churches and organizations could learn from these businesses to reexamine periodically their own activities to see if they have deviated from their primary mission.

Some sample mission statements are given at the end of this chapter.

The CEO

The board is responsible for choosing the right CEO—whether a pastor for a church or a leader for a parachurch organization or the executive for a charitable foundation—who can carry out the mission of the organization. The entire process should involve much prayer. The board needs to consider carefully the qualifications necessary in its CEO in order to carry out its mission. Realistically, however, probably no one will meet all the criteria. I have no idea how many reference forms I have filled out or how many references I have given over the phone. In the case of churches looking for a pastor, they want to know if the candidate can relate to every age group, be a great preacher, counselor, promoter, businessman, administrator, and on and on.

Too, churches sometimes think more highly of themselves than they ought. Once I was answering questions about a pastoral candidate over the phone, and the person on the other end of the line kept referring to the position as "senior pastor." I knew something of the church (though he did not know that I did), including the fact that it was not large and had only a part-time staff. When I asked what size congregation and what other full-time staff they had, he told me, acknowledging that there were no full-time staff except the pastor. So I asked him why he kept referring to the senior pastor. Actually, he was going to be the only pastor! I suspected that gave his church some prideful image in their own eyes.

But with all the questions organizations ask of referees, far too often is the most crucial question not asked: Is the person godly?

Having chosen the leader, the board must support, nurture, encourage, guide, and sometimes confront him or her. In turn, the leader will also educate and guide the board. This is especially true in the case of a pastor in relation to his elders and/or deacons, many of whom will not be as spiritually mature and doctrinally astute as he is.

The Succession

One day I was in the office of the CEO of the first business board I served on, and we began to talk about the future of the company. The gentleman reached into his personal file and pulled out a sheet on which he had listed all the important executives of the company and who could be the successor of each should that need arise with or without warning. He also said he updated the list periodically. That's good planning and sets a good example for nonprofit organizations, especially larger ones. Indeed, some businesses spend considerable sums of money on succession planning.

Evaluations

While everyone in a church or organization bears responsibility and thus accountability, the CEO and the board bear the most. Therefore, accountability is especially required of them. It is fairly common for a board or a committee to examine and evaluate its leader on a regular basis (usually annually), but boards are reluctant to evaluate themselves. After all, they represent the bosses! But the board is at the top of the pile of responsibility and therefore of accountability.

A board self-evaluation can be done privately and anonymously after a meeting with the results tabulated for presentation and discussion at the next meeting. A questionnaire should be brief and uncomplicated with easily answered questions. Most questions should be stated so each item can be scored on a scale from one to five. Questions might well include the following:

Mission
fuzzy _____ clear _____
poorly or partly accomplished
in the last year _____ well accomplished _____

Board working together
poorly _____ well _____

Board and CEO working together
poorly _____ well _____

Board leadership
mediocre _____ helpful _____

Board committees
ineffective _____ very useful _____

Fiscal responsibilities
sloppy _____ reliable _____

Interest of members
casual _____ involved _____

Overall, we are doing our job
poorly _____ very well _____

Is there a board member you think ought to be retired
or replaced?

What things do you feel need to be improved or
changed?

Such an exercise done regularly cannot but help a board be more faithful in carrying out its stewardship responsibilities.

Some Examples of Mission Statements

Here are examples of mission statements of various organizations.

Peachtree Corners Baptist Church, Norcross, Georgia —"Striving to be obedient to God's biblical mandate, we are committed to worship the risen Christ, to develop the believers for effective Christian living, and to proclaim the Gospel to our community and to the world—all to the ultimate glory of God."

"First Baptist Church [Dallas, Texas] exists to love and worship God as we introduce people to the Lord Jesus Christ, encourage them to grow and mature in their faith with an uncompromising commitment to the Word of God, and equip them for service through the power of the Holy Spirit."

American Tract Society—"To make Jesus Christ known in His redeeming grace and to promote the interests of vital godliness and sound morality by printing and circulating religious tracts and other publications of an evangelical character."

"Philadelphia College of Bible exists to develop for the Christian church and related ministries leaders who possess a foundational knowledge of the Scriptures and a biblical world/life view. Its educational climate fosters development of intellectual and spiritual maturity, leadership potential and a global perspective on mission. Undergraduate programs emphasize biblical studies complemented by general and professional education and field experience."

The stated purpose of Word of Life Fellowship is "the evangelization and discipleship of youth through various means consistent with the Holy Scriptures to help build and strengthen the church of Jesus Christ."

Baylor University Health Care System—"To operate as an integrated health care system which exists to serve people as an extension of the Christian ministry of healing by offering a continuum of quality services with a commitment to patient care, medical education, research and community service."

8

Organization of the Board

E very board has to have some organization even if the board is very small and has little to manage. Larger ministries do not necessarily require a larger board but may discharge their responsibilities by the appointment and functioning of various committees of the board. Some activities may only need a single board member to act as a liaison or board representative in relation to a matter. Too, the organization of the board should create and maintain an atmosphere in which the board can best function.

Officers

Every board of whatever size must have a *chair*. Someone must preside and direct the meetings. The chair also sets the tone of the board and its meetings. Presiding does not mean dictating, but it does mean directing. A good chair will have the matters on the agenda well in hand, will know how much time to allow for each item, and will move things along without stifling discussion.

The chair should in most cases serve for a limited term, then someone else will be elected. An exception to this is the organization whose founder is still alive and active and serves as chair. In every case, however, the chair is responsible for the board process. He or she must fairly and firmly lead the group in achieving the mission of the organization.

Boards generally have a *vice-chair*. If that person's only function is to replace the chair at meetings whenever he or she cannot be present, then the office is really unnecessary. If the chair has to be absent from a meeting or function, then the board could simply appoint someone to chair that meeting or represent the board at the function. If the vice-chair has other designated responsibilities, like chairing a committee, then the board may want to elect a vice-chair.

Someone must take minutes. The *secretary* does not have to be a member of the board, but can be an officer under the direction of the board. The secretary must be present to take careful and complete minutes. Consider having the CEO serve in this capacity. At any rate it would be well to have the chair review the minutes before they are distributed to the members for approval. Minutes are very important for legal and historical reasons, so this is an office that needs to be carefully filled. The secretary is responsible for the integrity of all board documents. Minutes need to be written in a formal fashion. No first names. No bare-bones content because people will not remember details that need to be part of the minutes. Years later and with changes in board membership, the historical record needs to be complete to be helpful.

A *treasurer* can have both figurehead duties and/or serious responsibilities. His or her name will usually be printed on the gift receipts even though someone on the staff actually handles those receipts. Any officer of the organization, however, could acknowledge gifts—it does not have to be the treasurer nor a member of the board. But the treasurer, if a member of the board, might also serve as chair of a finance committee (if the board has one) and a liaison with the annual audit (though again a staff member will usually be the person to work closely with the audit process).

Committees

First and foremost, every committee should have a defensible reason for its existence and a clear statement of its purpose and responsibilities. Furthermore, if a committee has no ongoing need to function and seldom handles operating items, it may not need to be constituted—some other means could be found to care for an occasional need.

Many boards have an *executive committee* that tends to become the real board within the board. This is done either because the board is too large or too scattered to conduct all the necessary business between stated meetings. The need for an executive committee may indicate that there are not enough stated meetings. Of course, there may be justification for having a larger board, in which case an executive committee may be necessary. But the potential downside is that the members of the executive committee become the "in" group, which in turn may result in a corresponding lessening of interest on the part of directors who are not members of the executive committee.

Notice how interwoven these matters are. Size and geographical distribution of the board may affect the number of meetings (a large and widely dispersed board generally results in a decreased number of meetings), and fewer meetings will give rise to an executive committee, which in turn creates an insider/outsider dichotomy on the board, which in turn may result in the executive committee becoming too involved in managing.

> When not established because of board size, an executive committee ordinarily arises because of a lack of clarity in the board's delegation of authority to the CEO. Therefore, executive committees (1) make or approve executive decisions that could otherwise be left to the CEO, (2) assume board prerogatives that should be left to the board, or (3) do both. In other words, executive committees authorized to act must take power either from the board or from the CEO. Establishment of an executive committee to make board decisions between monthly meetings is specious. Board decisions will not arise that often if the board is proactive and delegating properly.[1]

Some matters that an executive committee might otherwise act on can sometimes be approved by sending a written consent to each board member for his or her signature.

I personally feel that a *finance committee* may be more important than an executive committee simply because so much of a board's time is usually taken up with financial matters. That committee can be involved with supervising the budget, examining regular (monthly) financial statements, overseeing the audit, proposing policies with regard to finances, and seeing that policies approved by the board are adhered to. Regular financial statements to the entire board or at least to the finance committee are essential in order to make the members alert to an incipient problem or trend that could lead to something more serious and more difficult to deal with if not caught early.

A *committee on board matters* (a kind of housekeeping committee) could be charged with keeping an eye out for prospective candidates, tracking board members' attendance and involvement, overseeing an annual board self-examination. This may not have to be a standing committee, for all members should be alert to prospective candidates, and an ad hoc committee could assume whatever needs to be done annually.

Indeed, functions that may be thought to need a committee can often be accomplished by either ad hoc committees that exist for a limited time or by an individual board member acting as a fact finder or liaison.

The *committee of the whole*, which is just another name for the entire membership of the board, should be committed to: (1) Maintaining an atmosphere that is conducive to free, open, and frank discussion.

Steamrolling over members will only result in those people becoming discouraged and disinterested. Strong board members are an asset, but they must operate as team members, not all-stars. (2) Maintaining total confidentiality about all that goes on in board meetings. Too often have I left a meeting only to hear (often the next day) from an outsider what went on and who said what in the meeting. There may be occasions when a board member may need to seek out and trust in a confidant in order to get advice and/or an objective perspective, but in such instances the confidant should be carefully chosen and observe total confidentially.

Having delineated officers and committees that are common to boards, I nonetheless caution that everything be kept as simple as possible, the number of officers and committees kept to a minimum. If something is not covered, appoint someone or establish a temporary committee to take care of it, then dissolve the committee when the matter is resolved. Bureaucracies are not only found in our national, state, and local governments; they also creep into boards. Remember the KISS acronym: Keep It Simple Stupid!

9

The Agenda

A cartoon showed two executives walking together. Both were in business suits, but one wore a cowboy hat and had a pistol hanging from one hand. He said to the other man, "I once shot a man for not having an agenda. I ain't proud, but things moved along pretty good after that." I, and probably lots of board members, can empathize.

Good board members do not have time to waste. Therefore, meetings should be run efficiently and effectively. A properly prepared and executed agenda serves as the basis for seeing that this happens.

Who determines the agenda? Normally the chair in conjunction with the CEO. If the CEO dictates the agenda then the board has lost some measure of control over its own functions. Worst case scenario: the chair comes to the meeting and asks, "What's on the agenda for today?"

What should guide the agenda? Three questions will keep the agenda in focus: (1) What should we spend the members' time talking about? (2) Is each item a board (not staff) issue? (3) Has the board already said something about this in its policies or previous discussions?

When is the agenda prepared? Before the meeting and in time to distribute it to the members along with supporting materials that explain items on the agenda. Only in this way can members be properly prepared to discuss intelligently the matters that come before the group. Worst case scenario: no agenda or explanatory exhibits arrive before the meeting. Next worse case scenario: materials arrive the day before the meeting. Next worse case scenario: materials arrive two weeks before the meeting, for then they will lie buried on the members' desks and not be resurrected in time to study them.

How much time should be allotted to each item on the agenda? This cannot be decided precisely, but the chair can usually make a good estimate, place the estimate on the agenda, and make every attempt to keep the meeting on schedule. Only one of all the boards on which I ever served did this, but it was done with almost uncanny precision. Seldom did a matter go over the time suggested on the agenda. And yet I never felt that the discussion was rushed or terminated before it should have been. But I have been to too many board, faculty, and committee meetings when the discussion got out of hand and the meeting went on interminably. It is no credit to the chair to let that happen simply because he or she "wants to give everyone a chance to speak."

Should items be added or deleted during the meeting? Normally, no. But the majority may consent to add or delete and, of course, matters can and sometimes should be postponed.

What is the place of prayer at meetings? Certainly every meeting should begin with a prayer, but a season of prayer could well be the normal practice. If say fifteen minutes are devoted to prayer at the start of every meeting, then see to it that almost all that time is spent praying and not giving requests or discussing problems to be prayed over. A simple way to avoid spending the time voicing requests is to place on the agenda the list of requests and pray over each item on it. A closing prayer may focus on the ramifications of decisions that have been made as well as ongoing needs. Certainly there is no law against stopping at any point in a meeting to offer a prayer for some specific need and/or to express thanksgiving.

What is the principal responsibility that a board discharges at its meetings? It is to do board business. While that seems obvious, it is not always practiced. Too often, boards concern themselves with managing the staff's business. Boards should seek to do the board's job, not the staff's jobs, though the board may review staff performance to measure it against the mission of the organization and the policies formulated by the board. Be wary of "the analysis paralysis." That is, analyzing a matter to death to avoid having to make a decision.

What contacts can be made between the CEO and the board between meetings? I am not speaking of official contacts that arise from the need to decide or legalize something, but of unofficial, more partner type contacts. These are especially important if meetings are held, say, quarterly, but should not be ruled out as unnecessary if meetings are held more frequently.

Regarding such contacts, Dr. Stephen E. Slocum, for many years President of the American Tract Society, has very helpful suggestions born out of his many years of experience working with his board. He sent monthly mailings between the quarterly meetings. Recognizing the tendency to put aside mailings that threaten to take our time and attention, he stamped on the outside of the envelope "For Information Only—Scan and Toss." He included in these mailings items of general interest from the media, a summary of current activities of the organization for prayer and praise, and even humorous cartoons. The board members looked forward to receiving these envelopes and were motivated to open them promptly. Other contacts were made using phone calls and postcards. If Dr. Slocum needed to send something that required the board members' close attention between meetings, he placed that in a different kind of envelope and marked it "Important." These are great suggestions.

How important is promptness? Very. Begin meetings on time and as far as possible end them on time. It is not right to penalize those who are prompt by waiting for latecomers before the starting the meeting.

How should members leave a meeting? Saying it was a worthwhile meeting. That does not mean there was no disagreement expressed, nor that everything was smoothed over and everyone left smiling piously and nodding their heads in superficial agreement. It does mean that we wrestled earnestly with board business, had full and frank discussion, sought the Lord's will in decisions that were made, and parted with a sense of comradeship and gratitude for being able to share together in the Lord's work.

10

Faith, Finances, and Foolhardiness

Integrity in fiscal matters occupies a top priority among the responsibilities of board members, including church leaders whether they be elders, deacons, stewards, or directors. Scandals caused by sloppy finances should be seen as serious as those that result from immoralities. And there probably have been more scandals related to finances, though they are not so widely publicized. The entire area of financial responsibility, fund raising, internal controls on money, the place of faith, vision, budgets, and debt are crucial and continuing responsibilities of boards.

A Philosophy

Ultimately the board must assume final and full responsibility for the way its organization's finances are handled. It seems that boards are more and more delegating fund raising to the CEO, who in turn employs professional fund raisers. Some of these professionals have let Scripture forge their philosophy of money and the legitimate techniques for communicating needs to a constituency, while too many have simply mimicked the methods of the secular fund raiser. Regardless of whether the board takes on responsibility for fund raising or delegates it to others, the board must forge the philosophy that they or those employed by them will follow.

Years ago I served on a committee of the board of a Christian organization that sought to employ someone in this area of fund raising. We interviewed several people—some skilled in wills, trust, annuities, and other areas of financial planning; others in how to write appeal letters that would bring results. But the man we chose was one whose philosophy about money seemed the most biblical. He himself was a man of prayer who permeated his constituency with his ministry by making prayer primary in all areas of fund raising. He also believed that arm-twisting and guilt trips were never to be used. The committee felt he could learn about trusts, annuities, etc., but his philosophy was his primary qualification. We had no regrets about the choice.

Implementing the Philosophy

Too often there exists a large gap between a good philosophy and its (often worldly) implementation. The philosophy should be clear enough to direct what kind of appeals are compatible with that philosophy. What kind of appeal letters are appropriate and how many letters should be sent out during the year? Do we have a banquet to raise money (sometimes with a speaker invited because he is well known, not because he is in step with the organization)? Or a golf tournament or 10K run? Or an auction? Or a garage sale? Or a pledge drive (the season of stewardship appeal in some churches)? The board itself does not necessarily make all these decisions, but it should have a clear enough philosophy so that whoever is responsible for making them can do so unequivocally.

As fund raising for Christian churches and organizations has become more professional and sophisticated, it has also become more secular in its methods. Eliminate the Christian words from appeal letters and delete the inevitable "of course our primary need is prayer," and you could be reading an appeal from almost anyone.

One day I answered the phone and the caller announced that she was contacting me on behalf of Dr. So-and-so of a very well-known Christian ministry, and he had asked her to deliver this message to me. Then she read (not well) from a card in front of her the message, which was (naturally) an appeal for funds. Could Dr. So-and-so count on me for $50? I replied that I would first have to ask some questions. I wanted to know for whom she worked, and as I suspected, she was employed by a secular company hired by the Christian organization to make these phone solicitations. Was her company being paid a percentage of the money raised? No, they were being paid per call. I told her I did not agree with such tactics, and I hoped (in vain) that she would pass that word along to Dr. So-and-so.

Within days of that call, I received an almost identical one from a company hired by my U. S. Senator who was running for reelection. There was little difference between the "pitch" of the two calls.

Similarly, capital drives for churches that employ an outside fund raising company follow procedures that are very much like the annual United Fund campaign: similar schedule of dinners; similar breakdown into small groups with their "captains"; similar pledge cards. Just add some Bible verses and prayer to give a veneer of spirituality to the secular approach.

One year I kept count of the general appeal letters I received from three different Christian organizations whose mailing lists I was on. One sent seventeen letters; the second, twenty-one; and the third, thirty. Three years later the same organizations sent, respectively, seventeen, sixteen, and twenty-four.

Generally speaking, fund raising philosophies fall into three categories: prayer alone; prayer and information; prayer, information, and solicitation. I could not find a published, contemporary example of the first. An example of the second is this: "While friends are free to mention the needs . . . and information is always available upon request, our official policy is never to solicit funds. Rather, our expectation is from the Lord." This policy used to be published regularly in that organization's publications, but it eventually dropped out of sight and out of practice when that particular ministry began to do fund raising with the gimmicks and pressures commonly employed by others. Examples of the third are in almost every appeal letter one receives today.

Here are excerpts from what I consider to be a well-stated financial policy published by a fine contemporary evangelical organization.

> When . . . [we] were first organized over 20 years ago, I decided we would follow a 'pay-as-you-go' policy and the Lord has honored this throughout all these years. . . .

> When people ask how we finance all this [120,000 copies of a monthly publication, 150,000 copies of a quarterly publication, 310 radio programs annually, home office, etc.] we have to attribute it to the Lord, through the help of Christian friends all over the nation. We never employ fund-raising organizations, never use phone solicitations, never advertise for gifts, never buy, sell, or rent mailing lists, or use any of the other "gimmicks" that many organizations employ. . . . In addition, all speaking honoraria and seminar book sales . . . are turned over for use in our general operations. A few churches have us on their missionary budgets and, very rarely, small foundation grants and bequests are received.

> We try to follow the Biblical principle of paying every bill promptly, not contracting for anything that will compromise this policy. . . . We have, by His grace, ended each year just barely in the black, and we have never yet had to lay off any employee for financial reasons.

This is a policy worthy of thoughtful consideration in a day when so many Christian organizations employ many of the methods this policy forbids.

Incidentally, if you want to know if your name is being sold or rented to others, use different forms of your name (one initial or two plus last name, or full name, or middle and last names) when you subscribe to a Christian magazine or respond to an offer. Then when you receive other materials you did not ask for, you will be able to tell who sold your name by the way it appears on the unasked-for material.

A board cannot manage all of these aspects of fund raising, but they surely are responsible for reviewing them to test their acceptability as measured by the philosophy, not expediency.

The Budget

Undoubtedly formulating, approving, and controlling the budget is one of the most important responsibilities of a board. Nevertheless, the board need not concern itself with every item in the budget. One writer has suggested some questions that a board should ask in relation to their control over the budget.

"The starting questions for any board are 'What is it about the budget that we wish to control?' and 'If we were never to see a budget, what specific conditions would we worry about?'"[1] I think these questions may be more applicable to the budget of a large organization (including many churches), whereas the board of a small entity could well examine every line. Whatever scrutiny a board gives to the budget it must always be viewed against the mission of the organization, a set of priorities in carrying out that mission, and a constant remembering that the money comes in many instances from small donors who themselves live on a strict budget and who expect the organization to be judicious in how it spends their money.

To prevent bewilderment and thus disinterest on the part of board members who are not experienced in reading financial statements, budgets and financial reports should be presented in clear, sensible form (whether or not the form would be acceptable to a CPA!). The financial officer on one board on which I served presented succinct, monthly financial statements on one side of a single page; no one could miss seeing where we were financially. For another board the statements were so confusing that I finally gave a sample of the clear statement to the business manager and asked him to imitate it. For another the statements suddenly became so detailed that no one examined them carefully. When I questioned the need for such detail, I was told that this was the result of the new computer program being used. I insisted that they either modify the program or make a hand done summary of the printout that we could all understand.

Internal Controls

Certain "no-nos" become imperative for fiscal responsibility. Again, the board is ultimately responsible for monitoring these, regardless of whoever does the hands-on administration. Restrictions include the following:

1. Must not use restricted contributions for any purpose other than that stipulated by the contributor. Such contributions must be handled as a sacred trust.

2. Must not make interdepartmental loans without a realistic time limit for repaying and without the receiving fund paying interest on the advance made by the loaning fund. Why is this right since all the money in whatever funds belongs to the organization? Simply because the loaning fund is diminished by the interest it could have been earning if it had not been borrowed from. This is especially important if the loaning fund is restricted in any way, say a dedicated building fund not yet being used.

Not long ago I learned that a gift I had made a year or so ago to a ministry for a specific purpose had been used to pay general fund expenses and would not be replaced for five or more years. In the meantime, the project for which the money was given was stymied. So far the organization has kept this information from me. Such fiscal irresponsibility is unethical, unchristian, and perhaps even illegal.

3. Must settle payables in a timely manner. An elder must enjoy a good reputation from outsiders (1 Tim. 3:7) and so must the church that he leads. This applies to other organizations as well. One sure way to spoil a good testimony is to be slow or delinquent in paying bills.

Faith

What is the place of faith in a faith ministry as far as budgeting is concerned? Well, faith is part and parcel of every budget simply because a budget concerns events that have not yet happened. But to budget income that cannot realistically be expected in order to cover programs "by faith" is foolhardy. Why not be realistic about what income can be expected on the basis of the previous several years, and if the Lord sees fit to send more in, surely a board will have no difficulty in deciding what to do with a surplus! Pray about what the group ought to do, but whether or not the Lord (not gimmickry) sends in the money often will be an evidence of whether or not the organization is praying in His will. Faith can easily slip into presumption; presumption can easily place God under obligation to perform; and that can easily foster all kinds of fund raising pressures and gimmicks.

I do not see any Scriptural basis for the popular "faith promise" approach to giving, because it asks a person to determine by faith how much he or she can give from funds they do not have or foresee having. It seems clear that 2 Corinthians 8:12 contravenes the faith promise: "It is acceptable according to what a man has, not according to what he does not have." Giving (and why not include budgeting?), according to this verse, should be planned on the basis of what you do have, not on what you hope to have "by faith."

What to Do with a Large Bequest

Occasionally an organization will receive a large gift or bequest, which poses a different kind of responsibility. The board often thinks this will solve all existing and foreseeable problems. Here are some matters to consider if a large gift comes.

1. If there is debt, pay it off first.

2. Consider carefully whether the gift (assuming it was not designated for a specific project) should be better spread around to help various aspects of a ministry or whether it should be used for a single project.

3. Infusing an unexpected sum of money into a project or building often entails thereafter supporting that project at a new level of expense. Future upkeep must be factored into succeeding budgets.

I once sat on a board that recieved a large bequest. Many on that board were ready to solve immediately all the needs of the organization, but a wiser head prevailed. Following his advice, we invested the money temporarily, took considerable time investigating where best to use it, made ourselves face the continuing expense of sustaining the projects we would give to, and took our time (several years) in dispersing the entire sum. This procedure proved to be responsible stewardship.

Debt

I would prefer to avoid such a touchy subject, but how can one avoid Romans 13:8: "Owe nothing to anyone except to love one another"? Or Proverbs 22:7: "The borrower becomes the lender's slave." Should a board put its organization or church in slavery by going into debt? "But we have property and buildings that could pay the debt if necessary," is the usual rejoinder. Or a new building will bring in more people whose contributions will enable us to service the debt.

But property, especially church property, cannot easily be sold because its use is restricted. Whether more people will come and stay and give, whether or not there will be a church fight or flight is unknown. Better not to go into debt, which will not only keep an organization from slavery but will also keep it in step with the Lord's timing as He brings in the funds. To go into debt may make it appear that since God has not supplied the need you must supply it yourself by borrowing.[2]

Favoritism and Partiality

Fund raising too often leads to the sin of favoritism or partiality. James excoriates those who show partiality toward the rich and against the poor (James 2:1–10). But how often this is done today in relation to donors. Those who give much are made members of an inner circle, given special gifts and trips, seated in prominent places, etc. And the small donor, whose giving in proportion to his or her income is often greater, is not so treated or recognized. To be rich in faith is better than being rich in the world (James 2:5).

Prayer

In all the facets of fund raising nothing is more important than prayer. God knows our needs and He certainly has the resources. He can and will supply them in answer to prayer at the best time for the life and ministry of His work (and He is certainly able to supply them before the need arises).

11

To Whom Much Is Given, Much Shall Be Required

As in every aspect of the Christian life, the stewardship of serving on a board requires faithfulness.

- Faithful to appraise realistically the commitment involved if one accepts an invitation to serve on a board
- Faithful in promoting the mission of the organization
- Faithful in attendance and participation in the activities of the board
- Faithful to guard the integrity of the board and its actions
- Faithful in using only godly means of soliciting funds
- Faithful in allocating funds in accordance with the goals of the organization and stipulations of donors

- Faithful in the process of choosing a leader when that becomes necessary
- Faithful to prepare for the succession of leadership
- Faithful to observe the strictest confidentiality
- Faithful in giving
- Faithful in praying for colleagues and the ministry
- Faithful to exemplify and promote excellence in every way

It is not enough that a Christian organization operates merely at a level acceptable to the law. The Christian organization must be faithful to a higher law. Some examples:

(1) The law does not permit scholarship grants to be designated by the donor to an individual, but only given to the educational institution or the church which in turn decides (usually by committee action) on the recipient(s). The institution or church must not guarantee simply to pass the contribution through to the donor's designee. Yet many churches violate this law by receipting gifts as tax exempt (for student aid, for example) then simply passing them through, without formal authorization, to the individual whom the donor has designated.

(2) The law allows board meetings to be held anywhere. Yet some Christian boards meet in exotic places and charge it off as business expense. That simply

depletes the amount of money that can be used for the purposes for which the organization was established.

(3) Occasionally charities come under attack because their top officials are paid inordinately high salaries. Should those professing to help the needy be paid such salaries? I remember an executive of a retirement plan for pastors and Christian workers who pleaded in a Sunday sermon for increased funding from the churches these pastors served. It was a legitimate plea, for many retirees were not cared for as they should have been. But I could hardly listen to that executive's sermon, because the week before I had learned exactly what salary he received, and it was inordinately high.

At the beginning of service on a board, new members could ask themselves what they want the organization or church to be at the conclusion of their term(s) on the board. Since several continuous years of service would not be uncommon, veteran board members then can look back and see how well their faithfulness has borne fruit. And fruit is not necessarily measured in growth but in depth, nor in branching out—which often dilutes—but in keeping the main thing the main thing. To be able to look back with thanksgiving to God and with satisfaction for a job well done for what He has accomplished through the board and all involved in the organization makes it all worthwhile.

Some Legalities

There are a number of legal issues that boards need to be prepared to address.

Articles of Incorporation

The government requires nonprofit organizations to have articles of incorporation and a charter under which authority they exist and operate. These proposed articles will have to be submitted along with an application for tax exempt status to the Internal Revenue Service. Then the organization can legally receive from donors funds that are exempt from taxes.

Usually the purposes of the entity are very broadly stated to permit the organization to do all kinds of nonprofit activities (e.g., religious, charitable, scientific, literary, educational). That no activity will be permitted to influence legislation should be clearly stated in order not to jeopardize the tax-exempt status. The mission statement of the organization then limits the focus of the organization from among the many things the articles may allow.

The articles of incorporation will also give the trustees or directors broad powers with regard to the investment of monies. It also may provide for compensation for services rendered.

If desired, the articles may legally contain a detailed doctrinal statement and specify that grants may be made only to those who signify conformity with that statement. I once was on a board that, along with several other charities, received funds annually from a trust set up under a will. But the trust required the receiving organizations to read out loud to the entire board the trust's doctrinal statement every year and then vote their agreement. Each year we did that, but I wondered if one of the other recipients did so, for some had departed from the doctrinal position of the trust. Still, they took the money.

Provision for amending the articles should include the proviso that no amendment will jeopardize the tax-exempt status of the organization.

It is very important that the articles contain a statement concerning the disposition of the assets should the organization cease to exist. In order for assets to retain tax exempt status, I recommend that the articles clearly specify that in this circumstance the assets be distributed only to organization(s) that are in agreement with the doctrinal statement of the ceasing organization. I recall a church that disbanded due to demographic changes. Its founding fathers seventy-five or more years before made provision that the assets would be distributed among several organizations in that city, provided the recipient organizations (which were churches and schools) could signify agreement with the church's doctrinal statement. This was good stewardship, and the receiving organizations thereby carried on the original purpose of the church.

Bylaws

An organization also needs bylaws. These are the basic rules that are adopted to govern the entity. They speak to foundational matters for governance, and are not often changed, though they can be amended by the directors or trustees. Here are some guidelines for bylaws.

Content

Bylaws contain only items that establish the foundational and basic structure of the organization. They do not contain policy matters that are generated as the organization proceeds to operate. Therefore, bylaws should be brief and unencumbered.

Size of Board

Bylaws can specify adjustments to the size of the board of trustees or directors within the limits stated in the articles. As previously discussed, I feel that a board should be small. One simple rule is to keep the size to seven or less. Any number larger than seven needs to be carefully justified. Of course, this bylaw can be amended to increase the size of the board, but should not be done quickly or lightly, and certainly not because someone has a friend he or she wants on the board.

Quorum

One bylaw concerns determining the quorum. It is best to set it no lower than fifty-one percent. Anything lower may indicate that the board has had difficulty with attendance and is unwilling to deal with the problem, so the quorum is lowered to avoid a potentially unpleasant situation. The standard for attendance may be part of the bylaws or may be stated in a policy that the board enacts.

Officers

Designation of officers are part of the bylaws. The number should be minimal, but their job should be described.

Committees

The number and job descriptions of committees is best covered in the policies of the board rather than in the bylaws.

Fund Raising

A fund raising policy could well be stated in the by-laws, which would make it more difficult to change rather than if it were simply a board policy.

Provision for Amendments and Changes

This procedure should be spelled out clearly. How much notice, and in what form, needs to be given for a proposed change? Can the change be made by simply majority or, say, two-thirds?

With both the articles of incorporation and the bylaws, legal advice will be necessary. Articles and bylaws constitute legal documents and therefore must be carefully crafted.

Conflicts of Interest

Since nonprofit boards often include members who are connected with businesses for which the nonprofit organization might have use, issues of possible conflict of interest may arise. Ultimately such conflicts might threaten the group's tax exempt status. But they might also raise questions by some of the supporters as to the propriety of an arrangement. Therefore, when considering using a member's services or business, the board should contemplate whether or not it would be comfortable if the constituency knew about the relationship. Any possible conflict of interest should be fully revealed to the board, and if the board concludes it is permissible to proceed, the member involved should abstain from voting on the matter.

A policy concerning conflicts of interest might well be considered by a board to reassure donors and to protect board members and executives. Here is a suggested one: "Trustees and administration officials shall disclose in writing to the board of trustees any person to whom they are closely related or organization with which they

are affiliated who or which presently transacts business
with [the organization] or might reasonably be expected
to do so in the future. Each disclosure shall be updated
and resubmitted on a yearly basis."[1]

A section of the Texas State Bar rule on conflicts of
interest states the following.

> A lawyer for a corporation or other orga-
> nization who is also a member of its board
> of directors should determine whether the
> responsibilities of the two roles may con-
> flict. The lawyer may be called on to advise
> the corporation in matters involving actions
> of the directors. Consideration should be
> given to the frequency with which such
> situations may arise, the potential inten-
> sity of the conflict, the effect of the
> lawyer's resignation from the board and
> the possibility of the corporation's obtain-
> ing legal advice from another lawyer in
> such situations. If there is material risk that
> the dual role will compromise the lawyer's
> independence of professional judgment,
> the lawyer should not serve as a director.[2]

Endnotes

Chapter 4

1. James L. Fisher, *The Board and the President* (New York: Macmillan, 1990), 19.

2. Peter Drucker, *Managing the Non-Profit Organization* (New York: HarperCollins, 1990), 173–74.

3. Richard P. Chait, Thomas P. Holland, and Barbara E. Taylor, *The Effective Board of Trustees* (Phoenix: ORYX Press, 1993), 116.

4. John Carver, *Boards That Make a Difference* (San Francisco: Jossey-Bass Publishers, 1990), 222.

Chapter 7

1. Thomas L. Whisler, "Some Do's and Don'ts for Directors," *The Wall Street Journal*, 21 March 1983.

2. Peter Drucker, *Managing the Non-Profit Organization* (New York: HarperCollins, 1990), 157.

3. Don Wright, *The Effective Bank Director* (Reston, Va.: Reston Publishing, 1985).

Chapter 8
1. John Carver, *Boards That Make a Difference* (San Francisco: Jossey-Bass Publishers, 1990), 164–65.

Chapter 10
1. John Carver, *Boards That Make a Difference* (San Francisco: Jossey-Bass Publishers, 1990), 100.

2. For thought-provoking discussion of this subject see Jeff Berg and Jim Burgess, *The Debt-Free Church* (Chicago: Moody, 1996).

Appendix
1. *The Responsibilities of a Charity's Volunteer Board* (Arlington, Va.: Council of Better Business Bureaus, 1992), 14.

2. Rule 1.06, section 16.